Occasional Papers
No. 47

Capital, Asset Risk and Bank Failure

Linda M. Hooks

Published by
Group of Thirty©
Washington, DC
1994

Table of Contents

I. Introduction

Risk-taking is intrinsic to banking. Bank management concerns itself with earning an appropriate return for the risks the bank assumes. Bank supervisors focus on ensuring that risk-taking does not become excessive, thereby threatening the safety and soundness of the bank or of the banking system.

To address concerns about the effects of risk-taking on financial stability, the Basle Committee on Banking Supervision, a committee of bank supervisory authorities from the Group of Ten countries, drafted international guidelines for the amount of capital internationally active banks should hold as a financial cushion against losses on its investments. While these nations already had capital adequacy rules, the new guidelines established an international standard. The new rules, known as the Basle Accord, were proposed in 1988. They became fully effective in 1992, and have been adopted by at least nine other countries as their national standards.

The Basle Accord is premised on the belief that an adequate level of capital is important to ensure bank safety and that the level of required capital can be calibrated to portfolio risk. Thus, the Accord requires that banks hold a minimum level of capital as a proportion of assets, with assets appropriately weighted to reflect their risk. The additional capital maintained against investments that are considered to be riskier is intended to provide an added financial cushion against potential losses from those investments.

While maintaining adequate capital clearly insulates an institution against financial losses and having capital at risk certainly encourages sound management behavior, the analysis that follows poses two challenges to risk-weighted capital as the centerpiece of prudent regulation. First, reliance on a capital standard cannot be absolute because some banks with high levels of capital to assets do fail. Second, reliance on fixed risk weights must be viewed with skepticism because these schemes do not help in predicting asset risk.

In considering these issues, Section II of this paper examines evidence from recent U.S. experiences with bank failures in Texas. Section III reviews theoretical work on predictability of asset risk[1] and tests various predictive models. Section IV considers the implications of the analysis and concludes that even sophisticated capital measures like the risk-based guidelines are limited in the protection they provide.

II. Capital Levels and Asset Risk Experience

One way to assess the role of capital and of asset risk in bank failure is to examine recent experience in the U.S. financial sector. The Texas banking crisis of the 1980s illustrates the extent of protection afforded by capital and the difficulties involved in determining how risky bank investments really are.

Capital and Bank Failure in the Texas Banking Crisis

The decline in profitability experienced by Texas banks in the 1980s is one of the most pronounced on record. After a period of growing profits during the mid-1970s, bank profits declined dramatically in the 1980s, and have only slowly recovered from that trough. The return on assets for Texas banks fell from 1.08 percent in 1982 to -1.45 percent in 1987. Reflecting this financial performance, there were increasing numbers of bank failures, which swelled over the decade from 7 in 1982 to a peak of 134 in 1989.

The swings in bank performance were a function of regional economic conditions. Texas banks were vulnerable to concentration of risks because of the dependence of the state economy on the oil industry. The swings in performance also reflected the underlying financial standing of individual banks.

For all Texas banks, capital dropped from 6.4 percent of assets in 1982 to 4.5 percent by 1989. Not surprisingly, the capital position of banks that failed was decidedly worse than that. Two years in advance of their failure, those banks that eventually failed averaged a 3 percent capital-to-assets ratio while other banks averaged 8 percent. However, this difference in capital levels for failed banks is

Exhibit 1. Higher Risk Loans Held by Texas Banks in the 1980s

Loan category as percent of assets

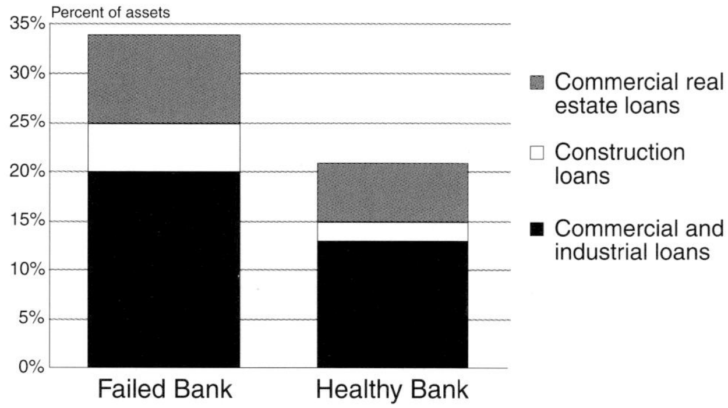

not evident from a more distant point in time. Before the onset of the Texas banking difficulties, the capital held by banks that eventually failed was similar to that held by those that did not fail. Ninety-five percent of the banks that eventually failed between 1986 and 1991 met the legally-required minimum capital standard in 1983. Almost two-thirds of banks that eventually failed had capital levels in 1983 that exceeded the required minimum level by 2 percentage points.

The same point can be made looking at the overall population of adequately capitalized banks in 1983. About 97 percent of all Texas banks met the legal requirements for capital in 1983, but 15 percent of these banks nonetheless failed between 1986 and 1991. Even capital in excess of regulatory requirements was not an absolute protection. Among the banks with capital 2 percent above the legal requirement, 13 percent eventually failed.

If a healthy level of bank capital was not sufficient to prevent failure, perhaps the cause lay in differences in the composition of the banks' asset portfolios. A look at Texas banks over the banking cycle, as the industry moved from few failures and high profitability to many failures and low profitability, reveals that failed banks allocated a greater share of their total assets to loans. Those loans averaged about 64 percent, while surviving banks averaged about 50 percent. They also held a higher concentration of their assets in loan categories—commercial and industrial loans, construction loans, commercial real estate—that are often identified as especially risky because they are all expected to perform poorly in a weak economy (Exhibit 1).

It is the question of the sufficiency of capital, in relation to the riskiness of the investments a bank chooses, that the Basle Accord is intended to address.

The Basle Accord

In 1988, the Basle Committee promulgated a capital standard designed to address the fact that some investments pose greater credit risks to banks than others. It was especially appropriate that an international forum should address this issue because an international standard would promote the competitive equality of capital rules among nations. Representatives of Belgium, Canada, France, Germany, Italy, Japan, Luxembourg, the Netherlands, Sweden, Switzerland, the United Kingdom, and the United States participated in this effort.

In essence, the Basle Accord attempted to accomplish two objectives: to establish an international minimum capital level; and to correct traditional approaches to capital adequacy for the variation in risk posed by different investments. The usual requirement that banks hold a minimum amount of capital relative to their total assets was augmented by introducing a weighting system. The Basle guidelines sort bank assets into four broad risk categories with risk weights of 0, 20, 50, and 100 percent. Assets in each category are multiplied by their risk weights and then added to yield total risk-weighted assets.

The category assigned a risk weight of zero includes cash, claims on the domestic central bank, and securities issued by the domestic central government (domestic in this case means the country in which the bank is based). The category which receives a 20 percent risk weight includes claims on other banks with a maturity of less than one year and cash items in the process of collection. The 50 percent risk-weight category includes fully-secured residential mortgage loans. In the 100 percent category are most loans, as well as claims on foreign central governments.

The four categories reflect the perceived level of risk associated with that asset class relative to the others. Thus, because securities issued by the domestic central government are considered completely secure, they have a zero-percent risk weight and no capital must be held against them. Loans are considered more risky, and most are assigned the highest risk weight of 100 percent. The three loan categories identified above as being important in Texas bank failures, commercial real estate loans, construction loans, and commercial and industrial loans, are all assigned an equal risk weight of 100 percent.

Under the guidelines, a bank must hold capital equal to 8 percent of its total risk-weighted assets. In establishing this ratio, policymakers also agreed upon a common definition of capital that corrects differences in capital definitions used by the individual countries. Amendments to the Accord are now under consideration that would add capital charges for market risk exposure of banks and identify—but not require additional capital for—institutions that face excessive interest rate exposure. Thus, the risk-based standards attempt to cover all risks and calibrate capital requirements to a bank's risk profile.

Do Fixed Risk Weights Adequately Account for Risk?

Although the Basle Accord attempts to promote safety and soundness of banks by matching capital requirements with a bank's level of risk taking, it is not clear that the attempt has been successful. The risk weighting scheme raises a number of concerns. The most widely discussed problem is the Accord's failure to encompass market risk arising from open positions in trading. This is being addressed by the pending amendments to the guidelines.

A second concern relates to the incentives the risk weights provide. Some bankers and policymakers argue that the zero-percent weight assigned to domestic government securities, in addition to being too optimistic, encourages banks to invest in government debt rather than lend to the private sector. A third concern is that the weights are applied to broad categories of loans without regard to

Exhibit 2. Portfolio Composition of Texas Banks

Loan category as percent of total loans

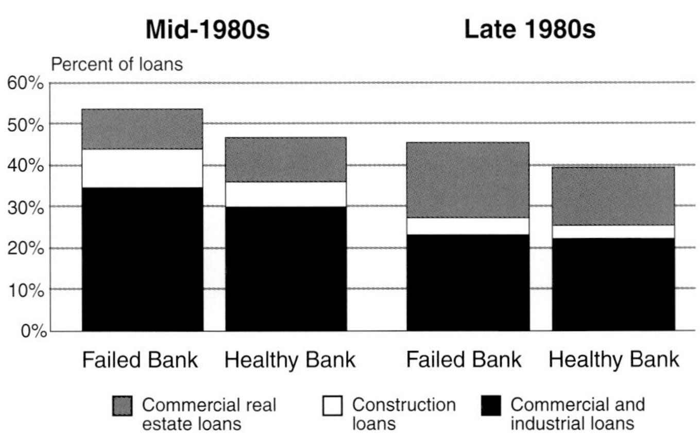

either variations within the category or the extent to which returns on individual categories relate to one another. In addition, the fact that equal weights are assigned to all types of loans provides no incentive to avoid riskier categories of lending (Exhibit 2).

Finally, the analysis in this paper suggests a more fundamental problem with the risk-weighting concept on which the Basle standards are based—that risk not only varies among types of loans but also over time. Some indication of this can be seen in data from the Texas banking crisis. The portfolio of a typical failed bank, in terms of the amount and mix of loans presumed to be risky, appeared very different at the end of the banking cycle than it did at the beginning. These data suggest that the relationship between broad categories of investments and the eventual probability of failure is unstable.

III. The Predictability of Asset Risk

Bank analysts have long used measures of asset risk in evaluating bank safety. Not only is the probability of losses from investments a critical determinant of bank survival, but asset risk measures are generally more forward-looking than other measures which tend to focus on past financial results. A number of measures have been developed for this purpose, with further discussion provided in the Annex:

- the loan-to-asset ratio, a measure of the share of loans in the portfolio;
- the Herfindahl Index, a measure of concentration of loans in specified loan categories; and
- the In-Sample Method, a methodology derived from finance theory that generates risk weights for each loan category in a bank's portfolio.

This section examines the statistical link between asset risk and bank distress using "early warning models" of bank failure. This will test the predictive ability of these measures and the theoretical validity of relying on fixed asset risk-weights to protect against bank failure. These models estimate the importance of various measures of bank financial health and performance, such as capital and income, in explaining bank failure. Using statistical analysis, the past relationship between these measures and bank failure is estimated. A numerical value is generated for each measure indicating its significance to the outcome. These values are then used to forecast failures in the future. The accuracy of a model is measured by the proportion of failed banks or surviving banks that it correctly identifies. Despite some theoretical limitations, early warning models provide valuable insights into the predictive capacity of various measures of financial health and performance.[2]

Most U.S. early warning models utilize similar measures of bank health and performance, typically based on the components of the so-called CAMEL rating used by regulators to evaluate the management and financial condition of a bank.[3] The components of the CAMEL are capital, asset quality, management, earnings, and liquidity. Early warning models often include variables to control for a bank's corporate structure, limitations on branching, bank size, and local economic conditions. For the reasons cited above, an asset risk measure is an important component of the models.

Asset Risk as Predictor of Bank Failure

What do the models tell us about the relationship between bank asset risk and the probability of bank failure? The U.S. banking sector is especially useful for examining these questions because it experienced an unusually high level of bank failures for an extended period during the 1980s. The high number of failures sharpens the identification of the relationship between asset risk and bank failure. The extended time period allows repeated estimation of the early warning models over several years, which permits exploration of the stability of the asset risk-failure relationship.

To test the predictive ability of asset risk, a series of estimations were done with early warning models. Every model included measures of equity capital, asset quality, management expertise, earnings, liquidity, and additional variables to control for other influences on bank failure. These include the bank's corporate structure, size, access to core deposits,[4] as well as the impact of local economic conditions. The asset risk measures were varied from model to model to test their utility. These variables are based on data from all U.S. insured commercial banks between 1985 and 1991, which captures the trough in the most recent U.S. banking cycle.[5]

One result of the analysis was that the traditional measures—the loan-to-asset ratio and the Herfindahl Index—were shown to be poor indicators of risk. As shown in Exhibit 3, the link between either measure and bank failure weakened as the banking cycle deepened; at times, both measures were negatively linked to bank failure. The In-Sample asset risk measure was more helpful because it contributed both more detailed information about asset categories and it showed that a number of the loan-category components were both strongly and consistently related to the probability of bank failure. However, this method also demonstrated some inconsistency.

Exhibit 3. The Link Between Failure and Asset Risk

Percent increase (decrease) in the probability of bank failure with a one percent increase in the asset risk measure

Asset Measure	Mid-1980s	1989
Loan-to-asset ratio	0.6%	0.1%
Herfindahl Index	0.2	0.1
In-Sample Method		
Commercial and Industrial Loans	1.2	0.5
Agricultural Loans	1.4	(0.3)
Commercial Real Estate Loans	0.2	0.6

Using the In-Sample Method, neither residential real estate loans nor construction loans (often considered a risky loan category) were found to contribute significantly to the probability of bank failure based on any of the models estimated.[6] On the other hand, portfolio components that contributed significantly to the likelihood of bank failure in at least one year in the repeated model estimations included commercial and industrial loans, agricultural production loans, consumer loans, loans to foreign governments, and commercial real estate loans. However, the impact of commercial and industrial loans and commercial real estate loans was unstable over the banking cycle, decreasing in the former case and increasing in the latter. At the same time, agricultural production loans became slightly negatively related to bank failure.

While it is interesting to see how individual risk measures performed, the more significant test of asset risk as a predictor of bank failure is whether the predictive accuracy of the models is improved if measures of asset risk are included. This was accomplished by comparing the predictive ability of models that used various asset risk measures to predictions of a benchmark model that included all explanatory variables except an asset risk measure (Exhibit 4). Not surprisingly, given the preceding discussion, the error rates for early warning models varied depending on the asset risk measure used and the time period chosen.

Exhibit 4. Error Rates of Early Warning Models[7]

Percent of banks misclassified as failed

Asset Measure	Mid-1980s	1989
In-Sample Method	25%	10%
Herfindahl Index	32	10
Benchmark (No Measure)	40	10

These results raise serious doubts about the value of asset risk measures in predicting bank failure. In the early going, asset risk matters: the more detailed In-Sample measure of asset risk has a lower error rate, and errors in predicting bank failure occur more frequently if asset risk is ignored. However, even the most sophisticated of the asset risk measures produces a sizable number of errors and is not a very reliable predictor of bank failure. Late in the cycle, asset risk measures add nothing to predictive capacity. Errors in predicting bank failures in later periods often occur equally whether asset risk is included or ignored.

The relative decrease late in the banking cycle in the predictive power of the forward-looking asset risk measures suggest that asset risk that was predicted in the earlier periods has now been incorporated more fully into bank capital ratios through loan write-downs. The equalization of performance among models that occurs late in the cycle similarly suggests that other less forward-looking performance variables have now captured past risk positions. Thus, the models using this improved information have greater predictive power.

Unfortunately, these findings suggest that even the most elaborately conceived asset risk measures are not very useful in predicting potential problems. Before a bank's problems become obvious, even sophisticated measures of asset risk do not identify potential problems very accurately because they cannot summarize all the factors that influence potential risk. And once difficulties are well under way, sophisticated asset risk measures do not add significantly to the information conveyed by traditional measures of bank health.

In order to form a definitive judgment about the Basle risk-weighting scheme, it would be useful to test the predictive ability of the Basle asset risk weights by running a series of estimations using early warning models. Unfortunately, precise estimation is not possible because the data available for the period preceding the adoption of the Basle Accord is not aggregated by the Accord's risk weight categories. However, a reasonable proxy is available for the Basle capital standard in the form of the loan-to-asset ratio.

As discussed above, the Basle Accord assigns the same risk value of 100 percent to most loans which is essentially what the loan-to-asset ratio does. While this ratio is not a perfect proxy, even if rough adjustments are made to reflect lower Basle weightings for certain categories of assets (within the limitations of the data), the results are nearly identical to those generated by the loan-to-asset ratio. Even if the fully elaborated Basle categories were to perform somewhat better than the loan-to-asset ratio as a predictor, the risk categories would still be less specific than those in the In-sample method and, like models using the loan-to-asset measure, likely to produce less reliable predictions of bank failure than models using the In-sample methodology. The conclusion remains that asset risk measures, including the Basle methodology, are unlikely to be useful in predicting potential problems for banks.

IV. Implications for Risk-Based Capital Standards

It is obvious that losses on risky bank assets can lead to bank failure and that capital provides a cushion against such losses. The fact that surviving banks in Texas weathered difficult times with higher capital than banks that eventually failed is an endorsement for the basic higher capital objectives of the Basle Accord.

At the same time, the evidence from Texas demonstrates that even above-average capitalization is no guarantee of solvency. Well capitalized banks fail, presumably because of the higher risks they have assumed. This problem the Basle Accord addresses by attempting to calibrate capital requirements to the riskiness of a bank's portfolio of assets.

On this point, the Texas data and statistical analysis of early warning models suggest that it is impossible, based on current techniques, to predict reliably the future risk of various classes of assets. The risk measures available have weak predictive ability and they are unstable over time. Therefore, capital standards based on these fixed asset weights will be imprecise and the protection provided against bank failure uncertain.

It is also clear that any risk measure based on broad asset categories can only be a general indicator of risk, since a single asset category such as commercial and industrial loans will contain assets of widely differing risk characteristics and quality. Also, risks for individual loans will change over time and, for similar loans, across locations.

Can a regulatory scheme be devised to adequately address these deficiencies? It is difficult to imagine a reporting system, however sophisticated, that is likely to pinpoint adequately the many sources of uncertainty, specific both to time and location, nor to identify consistently the changes in these sources.

All the evidence suggests that no capital standard can provide complete protection from bank failure. And a risk-based capital standard based on fixed asset classes will provide little additional protection from bank failure compared to a traditional measure of bank capital. While adequate capital is an important component of ensuring bank safety, it cannot be relied on exclusively.

Endnotes

[1] Asset risk is the risk that a counterparty could fail to live up to its obligations and a bank suffer a loss as a result. It is the same as credit risk.

[2] Early warning models lack a strong basis in economic theory. Just as there is no completely satisfactory theory of bank failure, there is little basis for the notion that statistical analysis of accounting measures should explain the probability of a bank's failure. The accounting measures are also a problem because econometric analysis proceeds from the assumption that the explanatory variables are independent of the outcome being explained. It is unlikely that this is the case and it is difficult to effectively control for this problem of feedback, or simultaneity. Several economists have developed early warning models that address simultaneity problems but these models have focused on the distinction between a bank's economic failure and its announced, or regulator-determined, failure. Examples of these models include Demigurc-Kunt (1989b), Gajewski (1990) and Thomson (1992).

[3] Avery and Hanweck (1984), Pantalone and Platt (1987), Thomson (1991), and Whalen (1991) estimate early warning models using various combinations of the variables mentioned. For a survey of the results of several different models, see Demigurc-Kunt (1989a).

[4] Core deposits are amounts in deposit accounts that represent a long-term, stable source of funding for banks.

[5] More detailed information on the estimates of early warning models used to generate the results reported here can be found in Hooks (1992).

[6] These findings support the arguments of Hall (1989) that the relative risk weights may be mis-specified. Bradley, Wambeke, and Whidbee

(1991) address similar difficulties in their empirical analysis of the risk-based capital guidelines for U.S. thrifts.

7 Errors arise in predictions from early warning models. Obviously higher numbers are worse. What Exhibit 4 says, for example in the first cell, is that 25 percent of the banks that were forecast as failing didn't in fact do so in a model which used the In-Sample Method of measuring asset risk when we looked at the experience of the mid-1980s.

All early warning models can all be summarized in a single equation with the predictor term on the left hand side—think of it as 1 when a bank fails and 0 when a bank survives—and on the right hand side, a string of algebraic terms. A model predicts failure by estimating the term on the left hand side. The estimates lie between 0 and 1. For example, the model may predict that a bank has a probability of failure equal to 0.6. To determine the number of errors that a model makes, a researcher must decide which estimates will be counted as predictions of failure. This is ambiguous because the researcher must decide which estimates are "close enough" to 1 to qualify as a prediction of failure. For example, the researcher may decide that an estimate of 0.9 or greater qualifies as a prediction of failure. The researcher then uses a cut-off point of a 0.9 to determine which banks are misclassified as failing and which banks are misclassified as surviving.

When comparing several different models, instead of choosing a standard cut-off point, a researcher usually chooses a standard error rate. This is because any chosen cut-off point (like 0.9) produces error rates for two different errors—banks misclassified as failing and banks misclassified as surviving. Both error rates will differ across models and it is therefore difficult to compare the models clearly. For example, if a researcher chooses 0.9 as the cut-off point, Model A might misclassify 10 percent of failed banks and 20 percent of surviving banks, while Model B misclassifies 20 percent of failed banks and 10 percent of surviving banks. Because of this difficulty, researchers usually choose a different cut-off point for each model so that one error rate remains equal across models. We followed a convention in the literature and chose cut-off points that produced a 5 percent error rate of banks misclassified as surviving in each model, and then calculated the error rate of banks misclassified as failing. That is tabulated in Exhibit 4.

References

Avery, Robert B. and Gerald A. Hanweck (1984), "A Dynamic Analysis of Bank Failures," *Proceeding of a Conference on Bank Structure and Competition*, Federal Reserve Bank of Chicago, 380-95.

Bradley, Michael G., Carol A. Wambeke, and David A. Whidbee (1991), "Risk Weights, Risk-based Capital and Deposit Insurance," *Journal of Banking and Finance*, 15, 875-893.

Copeland, Thomas E. and J. Fred Weston (1988), *Financial Theory and Corporate Policy* (New York: Addison-Wesley Publishing Company), 193-98.

Demigurc-Kunt, Asli (1989), "Deposit-Institution Failures: A Review of Empirical Literature," Federal Reserve Bank of Cleveland *Economic Review*, Quarter 4, 2-18.

—— (1989b), "Modeling Large Commercial-Bank Failures: A Simultaneous-Equation Analysis," Federal Reserve Bank of Cleveland Working Paper 8905.

Gajewski, Gregory (1990), "Modeling Bank Closures in the 1980s: The Roles of Regulatory Behavior, Farm Lending, and the Local Economy," in *Financial Services: Private and Public Policy*, ed. George Kaufman (Greenwich, Connecticut: JAI Press, Inc.).

Hall, Maximilian J.B. (1989), "The BIS Capital Adequacy 'Rules': A Critique," *Banca Nazionale del Lavoro Quarterly*, 169, 207-27.

Hooks, Linda M. (1992), "A Test of the Stability of Early Warning Models of Bank Failures," Federal Reserve Bank of Dallas Financial Industry Studies Working Paper 2-92.

Pantalone, Coleen C. and Marjorie B. Platt (1987), "Predicting Commercial Bank Failure Since Deregulation," *New England Economic Review*, July/August, 37-47.

Sharpe, W. F. (1964), "Capital Asset Prices: A Theory of Market Equilibrium under Conditions of Risk," *Journal of Finance*, September, 425-442.

Thomson, James B. (1991), "Predicting Bank Failures in the 1980s," Federal Reserve Bank of Cleveland *Economic Review*, Quarter 1, 9-20.

—— (1992), "Modeling the Bank Regulator's Closure Option: A Two-Step Logit Regression Approach," *Journal of Financial Services Research*, 6, 5-23.

Whalen, Gary (1991), "A Proportional Hazards Model of Bank Failure: An Examination of Its Usefulness as an Early Warning Tool," Federal Reserve Bank of Cleveland *Economic Review*, Quarter 1, 21-31.

Annex: Asset Risk Measures

Loan-to-asset ratio

The ratio of loans to total assets is the simplest measure of bank asset risk. The basic flaw is its assumption that each loan is equally risky when, in fact, risk varies by loan and across categories of loans. Using this measure, a bank with a high proportion of its assets in home mortgages would appear as risky as a bank with an equally high proportion of its assets in commercial real estate.

Loan concentration

Instead of focusing on all loans, analysts sometimes focus on the share of bank loans in a single loan category that has been judged to be particularly risky. Just as the loan-to-asset ratio is blind to differences in the performance of various components of the loan portfolio, this method fails to take account of any but the chosen component. Even if that class of loans does in fact generate volatile returns, a drop in those returns may be offset by an improvement in other components of the portfolio. In such cases, the return to the overall portfolio may be relatively stable, even though the returns to the identified category is quite volatile when viewed in isolation.

Herfindahl Index

This is a numerical index used by analysts to examine loan concentration across multiple lending categories identified as potentially risky. The Index is formed by taking the ratios of the total loans in the identified loan categories to total bank assets, squaring each ratio, and then adding up the squares. Thomson (1991) has found that the Herfindahl Index of loan concentration is positively related to bank failures in his estimates of early warning models on a sample of U.S. banks.

The Index focuses on concentration of assets in several asset categories as a measure of the overall riskiness of a bank's portfolio. However, because it focuses only on loan concentration, the Index also fails to account for differing risk levels or countervailing movements in returns across loan categories. A bank with high concentrations of loans in risky loan categories would be identified as having the same overall loan concentration—and hence level of asset risk—as a bank with a similar high concentrations of loans in a less risky loan categories.

In-Sample Method

This more comprehensive measurement technique, derived by using modern finance theory, measures risk by examining the components of the loan portfolio individually and by examining how the returns on the different components move relative to one another.

It is based on the capital asset pricing model which shows that the market price of an asset depends on the covariance risk of that asset, or how much the asset's returns move in tandem with the overall market's returns. According to the model, which is based on analysis of the stock market, the riskiness of an overall portfolio depends on both the share of the portfolio allocated to each stock and on the covariance of their returns.

For an individual stock , the risk measure *beta* derived from the model is a measure of the covariance between the returns to that stock and the stock market overall. For an overall portfolio, it is the sum of the covariance risks for each asset category, weighted by the proportion of assets allocated to each category. A formal derivation of the capital asset pricing model is provided by Sharpe (1964) while Copeland and Weston (1988) give a useful exposition of the risk measure *beta*.

The In-Sample Method does not involve the direct calculation of *beta* because data problems make this impossible for banks. *Beta* was developed for stock analysis and requires frequent (daily) observations on the returns for each type of asset under consideration. This information is not readily available for banks because most bank loan assets are not traded frequently. However, information on the components of a bank's portfolio by asset category is regularly reported to U.S. regulators. The In-Sample methodology involves addition of this data to a standard early warning model which generates a numerical value, or coefficient, for each loan category that has been included in the model.

The result is a risk calculation that includes all components of the bank's portfolio and allows for differing risk levels across loan categories. The values estimated by the model show the historical relationship between each asset category and the probability of bank failure. Each coefficient can be interpreted as a relative risk weight for that loan category, because it indicates the size of the relationship between that category and the probability of failure, holding other factors constant. Since this measure can include all asset categories and differentiates among their relative riskiness, it is an improvement over the simpler risk measures discussed above.

The methodology is referred to as "in-sample" because it estimates risk for each asset category from information included within the data being used to estimate the early warning model. An out-of-sample method, in contrast, would turn to an outside source like the equity market for estimates of the relative risk of each asset.

Group of Thirty Members

Rt. Hon. Lord Richardson of Duntisbourne KG
Honorary Chairman, Group of Thirty

Mr. Paul Volcker
Chairman, The Group of Thirty
Chairman, James D. Wolfensohn Inc.

Dr. Pedro Aspe
Secretario de Hacienda y Credito Público México

Mr. Geoffrey Bell
Executive Secretary, Group of Thirty
President, Geoffrey Bell & Company

Sir Roderick Carnegie
Hudson Conway Limited, Australia

Sr. Domingo Cavallo
Minister of the Economy, Argentina

Mr. E. Gerald Corrigan
Chairman, International Advisors, Goldman Sachs and Co.

Mr. Richard Debs
Advisory Director, Morgan Stanley

Sr. Guillermo de la Dehesa
Consejero Delegado, Banco Pastor

Professor Gerhard Fels
Director, Institut der Deutschen Wirtschaft

Dr. Jacob A. Frenkel
Governor, The Bank of Israel

Dr. Wilfried Guth
Member of the Supervisory Board, Deutsche Bank

Mr. Toyoo Gyohten
Chairman, The Bank of Tokyo

Group of Thirty Publications since 1985

Reports:

The Foreign Exchange Market in the 1980s
The Foreign Exchange Market Study Group. 1985

Countertrade in the World Economy
Robert V. Roosa, et al. 1985

Outlook for Mineral Commodities
R. H. Carnegie. 1986

Inflation Stabilization with Incomes Policy Support
Rudiger Dornbusch and Mario Henrique Simonsen, with discussion by Mario Brodersohn, Michael Bruno, G. G. Johnson. 1987

Finance for Developing Countries
Richard A. Debs, David L. Roberts, Eli M. Remolona. 1987

International Macroeconomic Policy Co-ordination
Policy Co-ordination Study Group. 1988

Perestroika: A Sustainable Process for Change
John P. Hardt and Sheila N. Heslin, with commentary by Oleg Bogomolov. 1989

The Risks Facing the World Economy
The Risks Facing the World Economy Study Group. 1991

Financing Eastern Europe
Richard A. Debs, Harvey Shapiro and Charles Taylor. 1991

The Summit Process and Collective Security: Future Responsibility Sharing
The Summit Reform Study Group. 1991

Sea Changes in Latin America
Pedro Aspe, Andres Bianchi and Domingo Cavallo, with discussion by S.T. Beza and William Rhodes. 1992

EMU After Maastricht
Peter B. Kenen. 1992

The William Taylor Memorial Lectures

1. **The Financial Disruptions of the 1980s: A Central Banker Looks Back**
   E. Gerald Corrigan. 1993

Special Reports:

Clearance and Settlement Systems in the World's Securities Markets
Steering & Working Committees of the Securities Clearance and Settlement Study. 1988

Clearance and Settlement Systems: Status Reports, Spring 1990
Various Authors. 1990

Conference on Clearance and Settlement Systems; London, March 1990: Speeches
Various Authors. 1990

Clearance and Settlement Systems: Status Reports, Year-End 1990
Various Authors. 1991

Clearance and Settlements Systems: Status Reports, Autumn 1992
Various Authors. 1992

Derivatives: Practices and Principle
Global Derivatives Study Group. 1993

Derivatives: Practices and Principles, Appendix I: Working Papers
Global Derivatives Study Group. 1993

Derivatives: Practices and Principles, Appendix II: Legal Enforceability: Survey of Nine Jurisdictions
Global Derivatives Study Group. 1993

Occasional Papers:

16. **Policy Lessons of the Development Experience**
Helen Hughes. 1985

17. **Japan's Role in the Emerging Global Securities Markets**
Hamish McRae. 1985

18. **Japan as Capital Exporter and the World Economy**
Masaru Yoshitomi. 1985

19. **The Dollar's Borrowed Strength**
Otmar Emminger. 1985

20. **The ECU: Birth of a New Currency**
Polly Reynolds Allen. 1986

21. **The United States and Japan in the International Monetary System 1946-1985**
Robert V. Roosa. 1986

22. **The Japanese Trade Surplus and Capital Outflow**
Michiya Matsukawa. 1987

23. **The State and the Market: The UK Experience of Privatisation**
J. A. Kay. 1987

24. **Adjustment in the World Economy**
Paul Krugman. 1987

25. **1992: The External Dimension**
David Henderson. 1989

26. **Japan's Savings and External Surplus in the World Economy**
Masaru Yoshitomi. 1989

27. **Reciprocity and the Unification of the European Banking Market**
Douglas Croham. 1989

28. **Financial and Monetary Integration in Europe: 1990, 1992 and Beyond**
Tommaso Padoa-Schioppa. 1990

29. **Implications of Increasing Corporate Indebtedness for Monetary Policy**
Benjamin M. Friedman. 1990

30. **Europe in the Nineties: Problems and Aspirations**
Wilfried Guth. 1990

31. **Two Views of German Reunification**
Hans Tietmeyer and Wilfried Guth. 1990

32. **Interdependence of Capital Markets and Policy Implications**
Stephen H. Axilrod. 1990

33. **Foreign Direct Investment: The Neglected Twin of Trade**
DeAnne Julius. 1991

34. **Privatization in Eastern and Central Europe**
Guillermo de la Dehesa. 1991

35. **International Trade in Banking Services: A Conceptual Framework**
Sydney J. Key and Hal S. Scott. 1991

36. **The Economic Transformation of East Germany: Some Preliminary Lessons**
Gerhard Fels and Claus Schnabel. 1991

37. **Are Foreign-owned Subsidiaries Good for the United States?**
Raymond Vernon. 1992

38. **Why Now? Change and Turmoil in U.S. Banking**
Lawrence J. White. 1992

39. **EMU and the Regions**
Guillermo de la Dehesa and Paul Krugman. 1992

40. **The New Trade Agenda**
Geza Feketekuty. 1992

41. **The Threat of Managed Trade to Transforming Economies**
Sylvia Ostry. 1993

42. **Tripolarism: Regional and Global Economic Cooperation**
Tommaso Padoa–Schioppa. 1993

43. **The Ten Commandments of Systemic Reform**
Václav Klaus. 1993

44. **Global Derivatives: Public Sector Responses**
James A. Leach, William J. McDonough, David W. Mullins, Brian Quinn. 1993

45. **The Impact of Trade on OECD Labor Markets**
Robert Z. Lawrence. 1994

46. **In Search of a Level Playing Field: The Implementation of the Basle Capital Accord in Japan and the United States**
Hal S. Scott and Shinsaku Iwahara. 1994